THE LITTLE BOOK OF
CHAMPAGNE

Published in 2022 by OH!
An Imprint of Welbeck Non-Fiction Limited,
part of Welbeck Publishing Group.
Based in London and Sydney.
www.welbeckpublishing.com

Compilation text © Welbeck Non-Fiction Limited 2022
Design © Welbeck Non-Fiction Limited 2022

Disclaimer:

ISBN 978-1-80069-202-2

Compiled and written by: RH
Editorial: Victoria Denne
Project manager: Russell Porter
Production: Jess Brisley

A CIP catalogue record for this book is available from the British Library

Printed in China

10 9 8 7 6 5 4 3 2 1

Cover image: Shutterstock.com

THE LITTLE BOOK OF

CHAMPAGNE

BUBBLY
PERFECTION

CONTENTS

Champagne
Etiquette

Champagne
Supernova

Wit and Wisdom

INTRODUCTION

Once served at the coronations
of French kings, wine from Champagne
is now popular around the world and
sales (mostly) increase year on year
(there was a covid dip but recovery was
swift) as people discover this delicious,
delightful, "de-lovely" drink. Although
true Champagne can only be sourced
from a small area of northern France,
there are hundreds of producers,
ranging from the globally famous
houses such as Dom Pérignon, Moët &
Chandon and Taittinger to the
thousands of family businesses and
cooperatives who produce on a smaller
(but no less delicious) scale.

Champagne is a drink with its own particular method that is carefully regulated. It has its own vocabulary, etiquette and above all, its own place in popular and culinary culture. Here, we look at the history of the drink from its early years to the present day and see what makes Champagne so very special. We delve into the intricacies of chilling (very cold), opening (carefully), pouring (a little, let the bubbles settle, then fill) and drinking (slowly). This book is fizzing with facts, quotes and information all about your favourite drink. So pop that cork, fill your glass and sip your way through...

CHAPTER
ONE

Champagne History

The Romans were reputedly the first to plant grapes in the Champagne region of France and the poet Lucan wrote of wine with "bullalae" (bubbles) as early as the first century BCE...

Champagne
comes only
from France...

There are four main growing areas of Champagne:

The Montagne de Reims,

The Vallée de la Marne

The Côte des Blancs

The Côte des Bar

... and seven counties:

Ardennes
Aube
Aisne
Haute-Marne
Marne
Seine-et-Marne
Yonne

319 villages

ARDENNES

SEINE-ET-MARNE

MARNE

AUBE

YONNE

HAUTE-MARNE

A Royal Drink

- On Christmas Day in 496CE Clovis was crowned king of France in Reims.

- From 898 all French kings were crowned in Reims, capital of the Champagne region.

- Joan I, Countess of Champagne married Philip IV, King of France in 1284.

It was not until the development of glass bottles strong enough to contain the pressure of the drink that sparkling Champagne became viable and desirable.

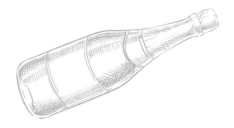

In **1662** an Englishman, Christophe Merrett, was the first to document "how to put the fizz into sparkling wine", in a paper to the Royal Society in **London**.

The monk **Dom Pérignon** – instrumental in the creation of Champagne – had so much trouble with exploding bottles that he named the drink "le vin du diable" (devil's wine).

The Science of Champagne

- Winemakers in Champagne wanted to produce fine wines like their neighbours to the south, such as Burgundy.

- Cold winters interrupted the fermentation process, causing...

• Sugars and yeast form carbon dioxide, which meant bottles could explode.

• Stronger bottles meant no more explosions and more fizz.

• The pressure inside a typical Champagne bottle is 90 hemispheres, which is the tyre pressure of a double-decker bus.

> **66**
>
> Our wine coopers of recent times use vast quantities of sugar and molasses to all sorts of wines to make them drink brisk and sparkling and to give them spirit.
>
> **99**

Englishman **Christopher Merrett** describing how sparkling wine was made in England in 1662 – 30 years before the development of Champagne in France

> **❝**
> # And make it brisk champaign become.
> **❞**

An early reference to sparkling (brisk) wine from the Champagne region – decades before Champagne as we know it was developed.

"Hudibras" by **Samuel Butler**, published in 1663

66

The English left these inexpensive still white wines on the London docks and the wines got cold so they started undergoing a second fermentation [causing them to become carbonated.]

99

Pierre-Emmanuel Taittinger of Taittinger Champagne, on the English contribution to a great drink

In 2015 the extensive
cellars , hillsides
and houses of the
Champagne region were
designated a UNESCO
World Heritage site.

Cellar master at the Abbé de Hautvilliers from 1668, **Dom Pérignon** originally tried to prevent the fizz in wine. However, he invented the "second fermentation" and was instrumental in developing Champagne wines to be the world leaders they are today.

66

Come quickly, I am tasting the stars.

99

Dom Pérignon (attributed),
a Benedictine monk – one of the earliest Champagne
developers in France

Champagne numbers

142 million
Bottles of Champagne sold
in France in 2021

25mph
Speed at which Champagne
corks pop out of the bottle

€4.2bn
Value of the Champagne
business for France

8.5%
Champagne sales as a
percentage of the total
wine market, up from
1.25% a decade ago

Protecting the Name

1845

Champagne producers went to court to prevent "Champagne" being used as a generic term for sparking wine from any other region.

1882
Trade body the *Syndicat du commerce des vins de Champagne* sat for the first time.

1941
Formation of the *Comité Interprofessionnel du Vin du Champagne.*

Following the death of Louis XIV in 1715, **Philippe II, Duc d'Orléans** became the French regent. He was a fan of sparkling Champagne and the drink enjoyed vast popularity among the nobility...

... This made the winemakers of Champagne produce more to satisfy the new demand that was spreading across Europe.

Madame **Clicquot Ponsardin**, known as the Grande Dame de Champagne, took over her husband's business in 1805 , after she was widowed at the age of just 27. Under her leadership the company – Veuve Clicquot – became an industry leader.

In 1917, Champagne was banned from Russia. The fall of the Tsars saw vodka established as the drink of the people.

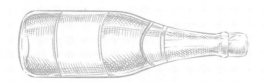

Champagne numbers

0.5%
World vineyard acreage represented by Champagne

4%
World vineyard acreage represented by France

15,000
Number of salaried staff
working in the industry

120,000
Number of annual
seasonal workers

The AOC (**Appellation d'Origine Controlée**) – defining where and how Champagne can be made – allowed the area increase in 2008, adding another 40 villages.

Annual reserves

- 250,000,000 kg of grapes
- The equivalent of 214,000,000 bottles
- The equivalent of 74% of a year's harvest

Champagne widows

As well as "La Veuve Cliquot", other women took over their husband's famous firms:

Lily **Bollinger**
Camille Olry-**Roederer**
Louise **Pommery**
Mathilde-Émilie **Perrier**

66

I decided there and then to carry on the business in my husband's stead.

99

Madame Louise Pommery – the inventor of Brut Champagne – upon learning of the death of her husband, 1858

66

I drink it when I'm happy
and when I'm sad. Sometimes
I drink it when I'm alone.
When I have company
I consider it obligatory. I trifle
with it if I'm not hungry and
drink it when I am.
Otherwise, I never touch it —
unless I'm thirsty...

99

Madame Lily Bollinger
(attributed),
1961

Sky's the limit

The years when famous comets are visible give "Comet Vintages".

The standout dates are:
1858 (Donati's Comet),
1811 (Great Comet)
and
1986 (Halley's Comet).

The Champagne process:

1. Pressing
2. First fermentation
3. Blending
4. Second fermentation
5. Lees ageing
6. Riddling
7. Disgorgement
8. Dosage...

...and then wait for at least 15 months.

Champagne numbers: how many bubbles in a bottle?

7,500,000
Gérard Liger-Belair, *Uncorked:
The Science of Champagne*

44,000,000
California Wine Institute

49,000,000
Bill Lembeck for the
Champagne Wines
Information Bureau

56,000,000
Karen MacNeil, *The Wine Bible*

250,000,000
Tom Stevenson, *Champagne &
Sparkling Wine Guide*

In **1910**, only 4% of the grape crop survived, meaning a huge drop in output. The reasons were varied: the phylloxera epidemic, flooding and hailstorms.

Celebration

- Great ships are launched with a smashed bottle of Champagne
- *Concorde*'s first flight was marked with a bottle
- When the English and French sections of the **Channel Tunnel** met, workers toasted with Champagne

Champagne numbers:

In 2020 exports fell:

-20% to the USA

-20% to the UK

-28% to Japan

-15% to Germany

But:

+14% to Australia...

2021 was a record year, however, with more than 322,000,000 bottles sold worldwide.

Bottles exported annually:

UK – 21m
USA – 20m
Japan – 10.8m
Germany – 10.1m
Belgium – 9m
Australia – 8.5m
Italy – 6.9m
Switzerland – 4.8m
Sweden – 3.2m
Spain – 3m

CHAPTER
TWO

Champagne Houses

From small family-owned firms and independent vineyards to multi-national conglomerates and cooperatives, there are many different types of Champagne producers and houses.

In Champagne there are

16,200 growers
4,300 producers
1,800 exporters
130 cooperatives
360 Champagne houses

The oldest Champagne producer still in existence is **Ruinart**. Production started in 1729.

Producer initials

These will appear somewhere on the label of every Champagne bottle, informing you about the maker and distributor.

Négociant-Manipulant (NM)

Someone who buys grapes or wine, makes Champagne and bottles it under their own name.

Récoltant-Manipulant (RM)

A grower who also makes, bottles and sells their own Champagne.

Coopérative de Manipulation (CM)

A cooperative that makes and sells its own Champagne from grapes in vineyards owned by members of the cooperative.

Récoltant-Coopérateur (RC)

Similar to a CM, above, but once pressed, the Champagne goes back to members of the cooperative, who sell it under their own label.

Société de Récoltants (SR)
A family group of growers who produce and sell their own-label Champagne from their own grapes.

Négociant Distributeur (ND)
Someone who buys finished bottles, puts their own label on and sells them.

Marque d'Acheteur (MA)
An own-brand Champagne that is produced for a single client.

The 17 Grands Crus in Champagne

The region's most important villages:

Ambonnay, Avize, Aÿ, Beaumont-sur-Vesle, Bouzy, Chouilly, Cramant, Le Mesnil-sur-Oger, Louvois, Mailly Champagne, Oger, Oiry, Puisieux, Sillery, Tours-sur-Marne, Verzenay, Verzy

A–Z of
Champagne Houses

The following is a little
A–Z of houses that includes
some of the most famous, best-
known and prestigious players as
well as a few independents and
tiny producers, and includes a
recommendation of wines to try.
This list is by no means
exhaustive – there are hundreds
more producers and thousands
more wines to try.

Barnaut, 1874
Ownership: Independent
Key Champagne: *Grande Réserve
Brut Grand Cru*

Billecart-Salmon, 1818
Ownership: Independent
Key Champagne:
Elite Blanc de Noirs

Boizel, 1834
Ownership: Independent
Key Champagne:
Grand Vintage 2012

Bollinger, 1829
Ownership: Société Jacques
Bollinger. Key Champagne:
Vieilles Vignes Françaises

Canard-Duchêne, 1868
Ownership: Groupe Thiénot
Key Champagne:
Grande Cuvée Charles VII

Charles Heidsieck, 1851
Ownership: EPI
Key Champagne:
Blanc des Millénaires

Charles de Cazanove, 1811
Ownership: Groupe Rapeneau
Key Champagne: *Stradivarius*

Duval-Leroy, 1859
Ownership: Family
Key Champagne:
Femme de Champagne

Nicolas Feuillatte, 1972
Ownership: Cooperative
Key Champagne:
Terroir Premier Cru

Ludovic Hatté, 1979
Ownership: Family
Key Champagne:
Brut Millésime 2008

Heidsieck & Co Monopole, 1785
Ownership: Vranken-Pommery
Monopole
Key Champagne:
Diamant Bleu

Champagne Jacquart, 1964
Ownership: Cooperative
Key Champagne: *Cuvée Prestive
Alpha Blanc*

"
Not just bubbles for
celebration, but a wine
that everyone loves ...
there is a magic behind
champagne.
"

Floriane Eznack from Champagne Jacquart

Krug, 1843
Ownership: LVMH
Key Champagne:
Clos du Mesnil

Lanson, 1760
Ownership: Lanson-BCC
Key Champagne:
La Noble Cuvée Brut 2002

Laurent-Perrier, 1812
Ownership: Laurent-Perrier
Key Champagne:
Grand Siécle

Moët & Chandon, 1743
Ownership: LVMH
Key Champagne:
Dom Pérignon

Moët & Chandon is one of the world's biggest Champagne producers and the house is most famous for its **Dom Pérignon** brand, named after the monk so instrumental in the creation of Champagne.

Mumm, 1827
Ownership: Pernod Ricard
Key Champagne: *RSRV Blanc de Blancs 2014*

Perrier-Jouët, 1811
Ownership: Pernod Ricard
Key Champagne:
Belle Époque

Piper-Heidsieck, 1785
Ownership: EPI
Key Champagne:
Cuvée Rare

Pol Roger, 1849
Ownership: Independent
Key Champagne: *Cuvée
Sir Winston Churchill*

❝
Champagne should be
dry, cold and free.
❞

Christian Pol-Roger

**Champagne Pommery,
1836**
Ownership: Vranken-Pommery
Monopole
Key Champagne:
Grand Vintage 2012

"

Joyful ... lightness.

"

Madame Pommery describing her Champagne

Louis Roederer, 1776
Ownership: Louis Roederer
Group
Champagne: *Cristal*

Ruinart, 1729
Ownership: LVMH
Key Champagne:
Ruinart Blanc de Blancs

Salon, 1921
Ownership: Laurent-Perrier
Key Champagne:
Champagne Salon

Taittinger, 1734
Ownership: Taittinger
Key Champagne:
Comtes de Champagne

66

[The English] invented the consumption of champagne … everything that's made the reputation of France in the world.

99

Pierre-Emmanuel Taittinger, 2019

Tarlant, 1687
Ownership: Family
Champagne: *Zero Brut Nature*

G. Tribaut, 1935
Ownership: Family
Key Champagne: *Grande Cuvée Spéciale 1er Cru*

Vilmart & Cie, 1872
Ownership: Independent
Key Champagne:
Coeur de Cuvée

Voirin-Jumel
Ownership: Independent
Key Champagne:
Cuvée 555

Veuve Clicquot Ponsardin, 1772
Ownership: LVMH
Key Champagne:
La Grande Dame

CHAPTER
THREE

The World of Champagne

Not only must Champagne come from a certain region, but the drink we know and love must be manufactured according to a strict set of rules...

Grape varieties that may be used to make champagne: Arbane, **Chardonnay**, Pinot Blanc, Pinot Gris, **Pinot Meunier**, **Pinot Noir**, Petit Meslier.

99% of grapes in Champagne vineyards are the three in **bold**

Only four methods of pruning are allowed:

Cordon de Royat
Chablis
Guyot
Vallée de la Marne

and annual pruning accounts for 25% of the year's work.

The
Méthode traditionnelle
(previously *méthode champenoise*) of production is tightly regulated to this day.

When first developed, the majority of **Champagne** was sweet, sugar contributing to the fizz. From the 20th century most Champagne was "brut". The term came from 'brute' – describing a wine made with no added sugar.

Ageing

Champagne undergoes ageing, during which the dead yeast cells (lees) break down and give the wine more flavour. There are minimum times for ageing, commonly from 18 months to 10 years (longer is better).

Blanc des blancs

A style of Champagne that is made only from Chardonnay grapes. Literally means "white from white", as in white wine from white grapes.

Blanc de noirs

This means literally "white from red", and is blended from Pinot Noir and Pinot Meunier varieties only.

Blending

The art of mixing different wines or vintages together to create a balanced drink before fermentation. *Assemblage* in French, this is a highly specialized job, undertaken by an expert wine maker, and the process is known by some as "where the magic happens".

Brut

The most common type of Champagne today – but it wasn't always so. Prior to the development of brut Champagne, which is made with a lower amount of sugar than sec or demi-sec, Champagne was a much sweeter wine.

Champagne houses

The most famous wines come from the most famous houses and there are more than 320 of these big producers. They may or may not produce their own grapes or wine, and sometimes they buy them from local growers. The big houses account for 90% of the Champagne export market.

Chef de cave

The cellar master at a large house. Probably the chief blender as well.

CIVC

Comité Iterprofessionel du vin de Champagne – the regulatory body of the Champagne industry.

Cooperative

A group of individual wine growers who produce Champagne together, either in terms of grape harvesting or wine production. There can be many members or just a few.

Crayères

Chalk quarries that were excavated by the Romans during their occupation of France. They are used for ageing Champagne and keep to a constant temperature. To be found all over the Champagne region.

Cru

(Grand Cru, Premier Cru, Autre Cru)
A form of classification of the vineyards
in Champagne. Contrary to practice
with other wines, this is done by village
not vineyard. Divided by Grand Cru (the
best), Premier Cru (first growth) and
Autre Cru (other). The Cru refers to the
rating, and Autre Cru is below 90%.

Cuvée

Literally, the juice from the pressing of
the grapes. There are various pressings,
starting wtih the first – and best (Tête

de Cuvée), to the final (rebêche), which isn't allowed to even be used in production of Champagne wines. It will be sent elswhere to be used in other drinks, for example liqueurs.

Demi-sec

A sweeter Champagne, made with a higher sugar content than brut or rosé Champagne.

Disgorging

(*dégorgement*) Following the second fermentation (see below) there is a deposit of old yeast that must be removed from the bottle. Dégorgement is that process, and was famously prefected by Madame Clicquot (la Veuve Clicquot) in 1816; it changed the entire way the wines were made.

Dosage

A mixture of wine and sugar that is added to a bottle of Champagne following *dégorgement* (see above). It is measured in terms of grams of sugar per litre. The dosage level determines the wine's category i.e. brut, demi-sec.

Fermentation

There are two different fermentations in the Champagne-making process. The first when alcohol is produced (and carbon dioxide is allowed to escape) before blending, and the second, following the addition of a sugar mixture, causing the bubbles to form.

Grandes marques

Literally the "big names" in Champagne, i.e. the major houses. Historically there were only 24 of these and they were the only members of the original trade body.

Growers

Récoltant-Manipulant in French, these people make Champagne that is produced on the same estate as the vineyards. There are 16,000 different growers in Champagne.

Harvest

All grapes are handpicked in around three weeks, usually in September, by a team of 120,000 pickers. The amount that can be picked is carefully regulated. *Vendange* in French.

Lees

The sediment in the bottom of a barrel or tank during fermentation.

Méthode traditionelle

Previously known as *méthode champenoise*, it is the strict set of rules followed in Champagne production. It is followed in Portugal, Italy and Spain to produce sparkling wines there too.

Perlage

The size, fizziness and texture of the bubbles in a bottle.

Phylloxera

An insect that destroys grapevines by attaching itself to the roots. It devastated the Champagne region in the 19th century, leading to wholesale re-planting. A tiny number of vineyards were unaffected and two still produce pre-phylloxera fruit, making Bollinger's rare *Champagne Vieilles Vignes Français* (VVF) for example.

Punt

The concave indentation in the bottom of wine bottle.

Pupitre

A special rack that holds a number of bottles at an angle of 35°, pointing down as they age.

Riddling

Remuage in French, this is the process of slightly shaking, tilting and turning the bottle every two days, increasing the angle slightly. Manual riddling is still used for finer wines (by a *remueur*) but mechanised riddling is common (with a machine called a gyropalette).

Sec

A medium-dry Champagne, sweeter than demi-sec.

Second Fermentation

See Fermentation, above.

Terroir

The unique identity of a particular site where food or drink originates. It combines knowledge of the physical environment with (in the case of wine) vinicultural practices to give distinctive characteristics to an area and its associated products. The Champagne region's unique traits and the méthode traditionelle combine to make a unique product, in this case sparkling wine.

Tirage

The bottling of a Champagne. When a year is mentioned in Champagne, it will be the year of bottling rather than the year of harvest.

Vigneron

Someone who grows grapes for wine-making purposes.

Vignoble

An area of vineyards.

Vintage (V)

This Champagne is blended from wines and pressings all from the same year, and aged for at least three years in the bottle. Non-vintage (NV) Champagne can be made from wines from a variety of years, and only needs to be aged for a minimum of 15 months.

Bottles

Quart
1/4 bottle

Demi
1/2 bottle

Champenoise
1 bottle

Magnum
2 bottles

Jeroboam
4 bottles

Rehoboam
6 bottles

Methuselah
8 bottles

Salmanazar
12 bottles

✄ CHAMPAGNE BOTTLES ✄

Balthazar
16 bottles

Nebuchadnezzar
20 bottles

Solomon
24 bottles

Sovereign
35 bottles

Primat
36 bottles

Melchizedek
40 bottles

Most Expensive Champagnes

(approx. per bottle as of 2021)

1 – **2013 Taste of Diamonds**
by Goût de Diamants ($2.07m)

2 – **2013 Armand de Brignac Rosé** ($275,000)

3 – **2011 Armand de Brignac** ($90,000)

4 – **1996 Dom Pérignon Rosé Gold** ($49,000)

5 – 1820 Juglar Cuvée ($43,000)

6 – 1959 Dom Pérignon
($42,000)

7 – 1841 Veuve Clicquot
($34,000)

8 – 1928 Krug ($21,000)

9 – 1990 Louis Roederer Cristal Brut Millennium Cuvée ($18,000)

10 – "Shipwreck Champagne"
(average $14,000/bottle)

Champagne Types

Non-vintage (NV)

This is champagne that is blended each year from a variety of wines and vintages. These are aged in the bottle for a minimum of 15 months.

Multi-Vintage (MV)

As with non-vintage, these Champagnes are blended from a variety of vintages and wines, but they tend to be blends of older wines.

Vintage (Millésimé)

These wines are created from grapes of a single year, and must be aged in the bottle for at least three years.

Presige Cuvée (Tête de Cuvée)

Usually the top-of-the-range wine from a producer.

How dry is your Champagne?

A sugary mixture (dosage) is added to Champagne before second fermentation. The amount is carefully measured and gives you the Champagne type...

Non-Dosé (Brut Nature)
No sugar is added at all.

Extra Brut
A small dosage is added, no more than 6g per litre.

Brut
For the most popular style of Champagne, no more than 12g per litre.

Extra-sec/Extra-dry

A maximum dosage of 17g per litre
Sec: This is medium dry, with a dosage
of 17-32g per litre.

Demi-Sec

The common sweet Champagne, with a
dosage of 32–50g per litre.

Doux

The sweetest Champagne, containing
more than 50g per litre.

CHAPTER
FOUR

Champagne Etiquette

Not only is the world of Champagne production a complicated one, but there are guidelines to follow for the consumption as well...

How to open Champagne

1. Remove the Champagne carefully from its storage place.
2. Take off the foil.
3. Remove the *muselet* (wire cage) and place your thumb on the top of the cork.
4. Grip the cork in one hand and twist the bottle in the other. You are aiming for a "sigh" not a "pop".
5. Have a glass ready to pour into.

Champagne is best served between 8 and 9 degrees centigrade (47-50°F).

Ensure your Champagne is cold: a minimum three hours in the fridge, ideally in a water/ice mixture.

How to pour Champagne

1. Tip the glass – holding by the stem – to the side and slowly pour in half the amount you require (5cm/2 inches).
2. Repeat with the next glass.
3. When the mousse has died down, fill to the required volume.
4. Repeat with other glasses.
5. Don't forget to put the Champagne back in the fridge/ice.

The ideal glass

The 'wide tulip' is the glass most favoured by professionals, for optimum flavour and bubble enhancement. A coupe is definitely a no-no these days, however nice it looks.

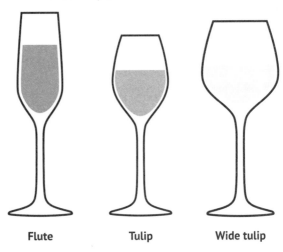

Flute   **Tulip**   **Wide tulip**

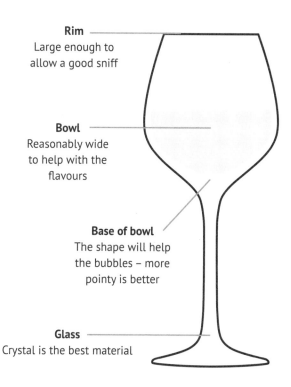

Rim
Large enough to
allow a good sniff

Bowl
Reasonably wide
to help with the
flavours

Base of bowl
The shape will help
the bubbles – more
pointy is better

Glass
Crystal is the best material

Sabrage

Napoleon was a fan of the technique of opening a bottle by sliding a saber along the neck to remove top of the bottle. Beware: it takes a lot of practice to get the perfect angle!

A **magnum** is ideal for a small Champagne party. It is said that the larger bottle size allows for better bubble development.

66

Unlike other wines,
Champagne has to be
kept standing in a cellar.
Once the Champagne has
been bottled, it won't get
better. There is no point
in keeping a bottle of
Champagne for years.

99

Julia Oudill, London's Compagnie des Vins Surnaturels

A **spoon** in the neck of a bottle of Champagne does nothing to preserve the fizz – you need a Champagne stopper.

Do

• Enjoy your Champagne, whatever its cost. It's about the experience, the company and the fun!

• Leave the wire cage on as you loosen the cork if you wish – it doesn't need to be removed fully.

• Hold your glass by the stem so you don't heat the Champagne.

Don't

• Swirl Champagne in the glass (Champagne battering). It will only reduce the fizz.

• Shake up a bottle and spray it – what a waste!

• Half-fill a Champagne bucket – it will only keep half the Champagne cold.

CHAPTER
FIVE

Champagne Supernova

The drink of Champagne has been featured in songs, movies and books, and has been the drink of celebrities for many years.

Marilyn Monroe drank Champagne "as if it were oxygen", according to her biographer George Barris.

Champagne brands with royal warrants

Bollinger
Lanson
Moët & Chandon
Mumm
Laurent Perrier
Louis Roederer
Pol Roger
Veuve Clicquot
Krug

James Bond movies featuring Bollinger

Live and Let Die
Moonraker
Octopussy
A View to a Kill
The Living Daylights
Licence to Kill
Goldeneye
Tomorrow Never Dies
The World Is Not Enough
Die Another Day
Casino Royale
Quantum of Solace

James Bond movies featuring Dom Pérignon

Dr. No
Goldfinger
Thunderball
You Only Live Twice
On Her Majesty's Secret Service
The Man With the Golden Gun
The Spy Who Loved Me

"

Maybe I misjudged you,
Stromberg ... Any man
who drinks Dom Pérignon
'52 can't be all bad.

"

James Bond (Roger Moore), *The Spy Who Loved Me*, 1977

66
Hey, did you ever try dunking a potato chip in Champagne? It's real crazy!

99

The Girl (Marilyn Monroe), *The Seven Year Itch*, 1955

66

Pink champagne – that's the kind of life we've both been used to.

99

Terry McKay (Deborah Kerr), *An Affair to Remember*, 1957

"

Henri wants us to finish this bottle, then three more. He says he'll water his garden with Champagne before he lets the Germans drink any of it.

"

Rick Blaine (Humphrey Bogart), *Casablanca*, 1942

❝

Whenever I drink
Champagne, I either laugh
or cry ... I get so emotional!
I love Champagne.

❞

Tina Turner

66

Champagne is the one
thing that gives me zest
when I feel tired.

99

Brigitte Bardot

Champagne movies

The Godfather Part 3 – Veuve Clicquot
Pretty Woman – Moët & Chandon
Moonstruck – Mumm
About Last Night – Perrier-Jouët
Once Upon a Crime – Piper-Heidsieck
Carry On Loving – Moët & Chandon
Jurassic Park – Moët & Chandon
Philadelphia – Dom Pérignon
Sons of the Desert – Piper-Heidsieck
The Great Gatsby – Moët & Chandon

Champagne songs

"Champagne Charlie" – George Laybourne (1868)

"Ruinart-Polka" (circa 1880)

"The Charles Heidsieck Waltz" (1895)

"Blue Champagne" – Glenn Miller (1944)

"Champagne Supernova" – Oasis (1996)

"Champagne Problems"– Megan Trainor (2016)

"Champagne Life" – Ne-Yo (2010)

"Spray the Champagne" – Migos (2015)

"Champagne Night" – Lady A (2019)

"Champagne Poetry" – Blake (2021)

66

Just yesterday I was
sleeping under a bridge,
and today I'm on the
grandest liner in the world
drinking champagne with
you fine people.

99

Jack Dawson (Leonardo DiCaprio), *Titanic*, 1997

"

I am honored to have been chosen as the Moët & Chandon ambassador and to make history with the brand, as the first celebrity face of Champagne.

"

Scarlett Johansson

❝

Pammy was gobsmacked.

❞

An eyewitness to Pamela Anderson's birthday gift of a 30-litre
bottle of Champagne, worth an estimated $195,000 in 2011

66

It is the most famous Champagne in the world; it's the most expensive Champagne in the world. Kim and Kris love the Champagne.

99

Kim Kardashian's wedding planner
on Armand de Brignac, 2011

"
Bubbles, anyone?
#champagne
"

Mariah Carey on Twitter, 2016

❝

Moët & Chandon has always been the Champagne of international trendsetters.

❞

Roger Federer, on becoming a brand ambassador

66

He and his crew spent $3m on Armand de Brignac...

99

Unknown source, talking about Leonardo DiCaprio's birthday spend
– all proceeds went to charity

66

Champagne, if you are
seeking the truth, is
better than a lie detector.

99

Graham Greene

"

Champagne with its foaming whirls

As white as Cleopatra's pearls

"

Don Juan, **Lord Byron**, 1819

66

If the aunt of the vicar
has never touched liquor,
watch out when she finds
the Champagne.

99

Rudyard Kipling

66

Champagne is like a
mistress. Sparkling,
lively, and capricious...

99

Eugene Onegin, **Alexander Pushkin**, 1833

66

Champagne is one of the elegant extras in life.

99

Charles Dickens

CHAPTER
SIX

Wit and Wisdom

A celebration of great Champagne
quotes, quips, sayings and more,
from the great, the good, the
witty and the wise.

66

Why do I drink
Champagne for breakfast?
Doesn't everyone?

99

Noël Coward

> **66**
>
> I only drink Champagne on two occasions: when I am in love and when I am not.
>
> **99**

Coco Chanel

66

Remember, gentlemen, it's not just France we are fighting for, it's Champagne.

99

Winston Churchill

66

The last explosions of the war were the popping of Champagne corks...

99

The German surrender of World War Two was signed
in Reims in 1945. Champagne was served at the celebration
afterwards – a 1934 Pommery.

Quote from wine historians Don and Petie Kladstrup in
Champagne, 2005

66

In success you deserve it and in defeat, you need it.

99

Winston Churchill on Champagne

66

We remain fully
mobilized to protect our
exporters, defend our
geographical indications
and promote our
agricultural excellence.

99

French trade minister **Franck Riester** on the row between France
and Russia about the labelling of sparkling wine

66

I preferred the 1825
Champagne to later
vintages we tasted, dating
from 1846, 1848 and 1874.

99

Serena Sutcliffe, head of Sotheby's international wine department,
upon tasting 1825 Perrier-Jouët

"

It was a memorable
evening, and tasting the
wine was like tasting
history in a bottle.

"

Wine writer **John Stimpfig** upon tasting the "world's oldest
Champagne" in 2009. The 1825 Perrier–Jouët was bottled ten years
after the Battle of Waterloo.

66

It was fantastic. It had
a very sweet taste, you
could taste oak and it
had a very strong tobacco
smell. And there were very
small bubbles.

99

Diver **Christian Ekstrom**, after tasting a bottle of Champagne
found at the bottom of the sea, believed to date from 1782.
(It was Clicquot.)

66

Only the unimaginative
can fail to find a reason to
drink Champagne.

99

Oscar Wilde

66

Too much of anything is bad, but too much Champagne is just right.

99

Mark Twain

66

My only regret in life is that I didn't drink enough Champagne.

99

John Maynard Keynes

"

Champagne is the wine of civilization and the oil of government.

"

Winston Churchill

66

The effervescence of
this fresh wine reveals
the true brilliance of
the French people.

99

Voltaire

"

The priest has just baptized you a Christian with water, and I baptize you a Frenchman, darling child, with a dewdrop of Champagne on your lips.

"

Paul Claudel

66

Champagne has the taste of an apple peeled with a steel knife.

99

Aldous Huxley

66

I'm only a beer teetotaller, not a Champagne teetotaller.

99

George Bernard Shaw

66

I'll drink your champagne.
I'll drink every drop of it,
I don't care if it kills me.

99

F. Scott Fitzgerald

66

Three be the things I shall
never attain: envy, content
and sufficient champagne.

99

Dorothy Parker

66

Burgundy makes you think of silly things; Bordeaux makes you talk about them, and Champagne makes you do them.

99

Jean Anthelme Brillat-Savarin

66

Champagne ... it gives you the impression that every day is a Sunday.

99

Marlene Dietrich

66

Champagne and orange
juice is a great drink.
The orange improves
the Champagne. The
Champagne definitely
improves the orange.

99

Philip, Duke of Edinburgh

"

First things first:
Get the Champagne.

"

Winston Churchill

66

Champagne ... the wine of kings, the king of wines

99

Guy de Maupassant

"

The feeling of friendship
is like that of being
comfortably filled with
roast beef; love is like
being enlivened with
Champagne.

"

Samuel Johnson

66

In a perfect world, everyone would have a glass of Champagne every evening.

99

Wine expert **Willie Gluckstern**

The most drinkable address in the world.

Winston Churchill on Champagne house Pol Roger

66

Always keep a bottle of
Champagne in the fridge for
special occasions. Sometimes,
the special occasion is
that you've got a bottle of
Champagne in the fridge.

99

Hester Browne

66
Life is too short to
not have oysters and
Champagne sometimes.
99

Christie Brinkley

❝

There is nothing more
beautiful than a sunset,
viewed over a glass of
chilled Champagne.

❞

Jared M. Brown

66

Not only does one drink
Champagne, but one
inhales it, one looks at
it, one swallows it ...
And one drinks it.

99

King Edward VII

> **“**
> He who doesn't risk never gets to drink Champagne.
> **”**

Russian proverb

Friends bring
happiness into
your life.
Best friends bring
Champagne.

66
Pleasure without Champagne is purely artificial.
99

Oscar Wilde

"

Gentlemen, in the little moment that remains to us between the crisis and the catastrophe, we may as well drink a glass of Champagne.

"

Paul Claudel

"

Start the day with a smile and finish it with Champagne.

"

Anon.

66

Wine gives one ideas, whereas Champagne gives one strategies.

99

Roman Payne

66

If life brings you troubles,
drink some Champagne...
then your problems will
just become bubbles.

99

Anon.

"

... if I must at some time leave this life, I would like to do so ensconced on a chaise longue, perfumed, wearing a velvet robe and pearl earrings, with a flute of Champagne beside me...

"

Olivia de Havilland

66

A single glass of
Champagne imparts a
feeling of exhilaration.
The nerves are braced; the
imagination is stirred; the
wits become more nimble.

99

Winston Churchill

"

Great love affairs start with Champagne and end with tisane.

"

Balzac

66

Meeting Franklin Roosevelt was like opening your first bottle of Champagne; knowing him was like drinking it.

99

Winston Churchill

KEEP
CALM
AND
DRINK
CHAMPAGNE